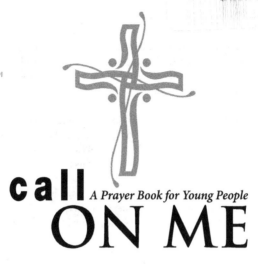

call *A Prayer Book for Young People*
ON ME

Answer me when I call, O God of my right!
You gave me room when I was in distress.
Be gracious to me, and hear my prayer.

Psalm 4:1

Jenifer C. Gamber & Sharon Ely Pearson

Morehouse Publishing
A division of Church Publishing Incorporated

Morehouse Publishing, 4775 Linglestown Road, Harrisburg, PA 17112
Morehouse Publishing, 445 Fifth Avenue, New York, NY 10016
Morehouse Publishing is an imprint of Church Publishing Incorporated.
www.churchpublishing.org

Cover design by Laurie Klein Westhafer

Library of Congress Cataloging-in-Publication Data

Gamber, Jenifer C.
    Call on me : a prayer book for young people / Jenifer C. Gamber and Sharon Ely Pearson.
        p.   cm.
    Includes bibliographical references and indexes.
    ISBN 978-0-8192-2834-5 1. Christian teenag-
ers—Prayers and devotions. 2. Episcopal Church. 3. Book of Common Prayer (1979) I. Pearson, Sharon Ely. II. Title.
    BV4850.G353 2012
    242'.83—dc23
                                                            2011050177

Printed in the United States of America

10 9 8 7 6 5 4 3 2 1

Contents

Foreword

My sons have always known a family dinner to be prefaced with the praying of Grace. We are Episcopalians and we do pray at home with predictable regularity. Reading, telling stories, and concluding with bedtime prayers was the ritual that marked the end of the day when my sons were young. When my oldest son was experiencing a particularly difficult week as an eighth grader, I discovered him reluctant to share his bedtime prayers. He gently explained that perhaps he was now too old to say children's prayers with his parents. I suggested that he could say his prayers by himself from now on. He thought about it a minute and then confessed that he didn't know how. I reminded him of the things we had talked about in youth group, about praying and meditating and reading the Bible. He interrupted me and asked if I knew where his prayer book was, the one from his great grandmother with his name engraved on the cover in gold script. I fetched it for him and asked him if he knew where to find the prayers he might need. "No, it's too long and the print is too small. But that's okay. I'll sleep on it," he confidently replied as he placed his *Book of Common Prayer* under his pillow and closed his eyes to await sleep.

  Call on Me is just the resource that I needed to help my son as a parent, to strengthen the teaching in our youth room at church, and to provide as a resource for youth and their families at home. This creative compilation offers simple and insightful instruction about prayer. It offers a wealth of diverse prayers on all manner of topics from prayers for the days of the week, to seasons of the year. You can find prayers to celebrate personal achievements and to address obstacles to grace and faith. Some prayers are ancient, traditional, and poetic while others are formed with fresher words of the current times; very straightforward and tangible. *Call on Me* is a perfect companion to *The Book of Common Prayer* for young people learning about their baptismal vows as they discern their readiness to offer themselves for the sacrament of confirmation. The prayer for the Death of a Pet would have saved our family from many a lengthy and painful backyard liturgy in which my youngest struggled through the Rite I Burial language, perched atop a milk crate, trowel in hand to bury an expired fish, or hamster, or newt.

I offer deep gratitude to Sharon and Jenifer who were motivated to create such a useful resource through their own faithfulness in prayer and compassion for young people. *Call on Me* will help equip our rising generations with a new tool to develop an active prayer life. Young people will welcome this resource as they practice praying for themselves and for others. I know that it won't be long before these prayers are offered as caritas for Happening weekends, as solace to friends who are grieving, and in digital form as messages of comfort, encouragement, and celebration.

May these prayers be our prayers as we strive to teach and nurture young Christians to be healers and advocates in a hungry and hurting world.

> Bronwyn Clark Skov
> Officer for Youth Ministries
> The Episcopal Church

> Advent 2011

Introduction

The apostle Paul encouraged his followers in Thessalonica, a town in ancient Greece, to "rejoice always, pray without ceasing, give thanks in all circumstances; for this is the will of God in Christ Jesus for you" (*1 Thessalonians 5:16–18*). These words are meant for us too. A pretty tall order! What about eating, sleeping, and working? How were we to fit those in too?

The way to solve this puzzle is to think of prayer as more than words. In fact, the catechism (*The Book of Common Prayer*, 856) defines prayer this way: "responding to God, by thought and by deeds, with or without words." We pray without ceasing when all that we do, all that we think, and all that we say is a response to God.

This book focuses on praying with words and is divided into three parts: common prayer, types of prayer, and personal prayer. Common prayer (prayer in community) gives us a rhythm to support our prayer, the knowledge that we are praying with others whether near or far, and the assurance that when we can't pray, someone is praying on our behalf. The section on types of prayer challenges us to expand the many ways we respond to God, whether asking for ourselves, asking on behalf of others, adoring God, or confessing how we have turned away from God. The third section, personal prayer, reflects prayers from our personal lives—with friends and family, at school and work, for ourselves and our concern for the world.

Most prayers begin with a verse or two from the Bible, which inform the prayers that follow. If the words in the prayer don't quite fit what is on your heart, consider looking up the verses in the Bible. Read them slowly a few times. Your own words may come. If not, God is praying within you. Listen!

The Internet has greatly expanded the community gathered in prayer. Sometimes it helps to know that others are praying for and with you. If you would like to offer your own prayers or pray for others, visit www.episcopalprayer.org where you can submit your own and read other people's prayers. You will also find additional information about prayer.

Writing and compiling these prayers filled us with joy as we remembered our own experiences as young people, noticed God's work in our lives, and thought of the young people in our lives today. Those who gave treasured time to review these prayers and make suggestions expanded our joy. Emily Gamber, a student at Wellesley College, and Andrew Kellner, Canon for Youth Ministry for the Diocese of Pennsylvania, provided particular insight and recommendations. We would also like to thank our families, particularly our spouses, Ed and John, for their patience during our hours of writing.

While this book offers prayers with words, in praying, we can hear God's voice calling us to take action. As you deepen your prayer practice, you may be surprised that you are "praying without ceasing."

Jenifer C. Gamber, schc & Sharon Ely Pearson
Advent 2011

COMMON PRAYER

Give us each day our daily bread.
Luke 11:3

Prayer is a way of responding to God's love and blessings. There are many ways to pray—with words, by actions, alone, with friends, or with your church community. You can even pray together with others across the world.

In the Episcopal Church, we have *The Book of Common Prayer*, a collection of worship services and prayers that everyone in the church can say together. That's why we call it "common prayer." When we come together to worship with others, we are following Jesus' example, "For when two or three are gathered in my name, I am there among them" (*Matthew 18:20*).

The Episcopal Church has worshipped with a *Book of Common Prayer* for nearly five hundred years. Thomas Cranmer, a church leader in England, compiled the first Anglican prayer book in 1549. The English language has changed a lot since then and so has *The Book of Common Prayer*. Even though the one we use today is from 1979, new prayers are written all the time. You can find some in new books called *Enriching Our Worship* and even on the Internet. All are written for the same basic reason: so that as a people of God we can pray and worship together.

No matter where you are, when you pray these common prayers, you are not alone. You are praying with many others around the world as one body with Christ.

Daily Devotions

It is good to give thanks to the Lord,
to sing praises to your name, O Most High;
to declare your steadfast love in the morning,
and your faithfulness by night.
    Psalm 92:1–2

Devotions are ways that we can pray along with reading the Bible. You can say devotions any time of the day. One tradition is to pray at fixed hours such as 6 a.m., 9 a.m., noon, 3 p.m., and so on. A schedule for prayer is called the *horaria*. Choosing a fixed time to pray each day establishes a familiar rhythm, which will help you maintain your practice even on those days you don't feel like praying. If you've chosen to pray when you wake up each morning at 6 a.m., your body and mind will remind you, "It's time to pray." It's like eating regularly. If you're used to eating dinner at 6 o'clock, your stomach starts growling at about 5:30. Your body reminds you that it's time to eat. The same is true for your soul.

You can choose your own *horaria* based on your schedule during the year. It might be different during the school year than during the summertime or when you are at camp. Consider praying in the same place or in the same posture. Our memories reside in our thoughts as well as our bodies. Are you used to kneeling during prayer at church? You might find kneeling to be a good way to focus on prayer. Some people have a special chair or corner of their room for prayer. You can create your own place by keeping your Bible and gathering items that remind you of God on your desk, dresser, or small table. By praying every day we can develop a stronger relationship with God.

The devotions here are from *The Book of Common Prayer*. What's neat about these prayers is that other people are saying these very same words—people in your own town or city, across the country, and even in other countries. Once you've established your practice, you might try writing your own devotions.

In the Morning

From Psalm 51

Open my lips, O Lord, *
    and my mouth shall proclaim your praise.
Create in me a clean heart, O God, *
    and renew a right spirit within me.
Cast me not away from your presence *
    and take not your holy Spirit from me.
Give me the joy of your saving help again *
    and sustain me with your bountiful Spirit.
Glory to the Father, and to the Son, and to the Holy Spirit: *
    as it was in the beginning, is now, and will be for ever. *Amen.*

A Reading

Blessed be the God and Father of our Lord Jesus Christ!
By his great mercy we have been born anew to a living hope
through the resurrection of Jesus Christ from the dead.
1 Peter 1:3

A period of silence may follow.

A hymn or canticle may be used; the Apostles' Creed may be said.

The Apostles' Creed

I believe in God, the Father almighty,
>   creator of heaven and earth;
I believe in Jesus Christ, his only Son, our Lord.
>   He was conceived by the power of the Holy Spirit
>   and born of the Virgin Mary.
>   He suffered under Pontius Pilate,
>   was crucified, died, and was buried.
>   He descended to the dead.
>   On the third day he rose again.
>   He ascended into heaven,
>   and is seated at the right hand of the Father.
>   He will come again to judge the living and the dead.
I believe in the Holy Spirit,
>   the holy catholic Church,
>   the communion of saints,
>   the forgiveness of sins,
>   the resurrection of the body,
>   and the life everlasting. *Amen.*

Prayers and thanksgivings may be offered for ourselves and others.

For whom and what shall we pray? For what shall we give thanks?

Offer prayers and thanksgivings silently or aloud.

The Lord's Prayer

Our Father, who art in heaven,
  hallowed be thy Name,
  thy kingdom come,
  thy will be done,
    on earth as it is in heaven.
Give us this day our daily bread.
And forgive us our trespasses,
  as we forgive those
    who trespass against us.
And lead us not into temptation,
  but deliver us from evil.

Our Father in heaven,
  hallowed be your Name,
  your kingdom come,
  your will be done,
    on earth as in heaven.
Give us today our daily bread.
Forgive us our sins
  as we forgive those
    who sin against us.
Save us from the time of trial,
  and deliver us from evil.

The Collect

Lord God, almighty and everlasting Father, you have brought us
in safety to this new day: Preserve us with your mighty power,
that we may not fall into sin, nor be overcome by adversity; and
in all we do, direct us to the fulfilling of your purpose; through
Jesus Christ our Lord. *Amen.*

At the Close of Day

Psalm 134

Behold now, bless the LORD, all you servants of the LORD, *
    you that stand by night in the house of the LORD.
Lift up your hands in the holy place and bless the LORD; *
    the LORD who made heaven and earth bless you out of Zion.

A Reading

Lord, you are in the midst of us and we are called by your Name:
Do not forsake us, O Lord our God.
Jeremiah 14:9, 22

The following may be said

Lord, you now have set your servant free *
    to go in peace as you have promised;
For these eyes of mine have seen the Savior, *
    whom you have prepared for all the world to see;
A Light to enlighten the nations, *
    and the glory of your people Israel.

Prayers and thanksgivings for yourself and others may follow. It is appropriate that prayers of thanksgiving for the blessings of the day, and penitence for our sins, be included.

The Lord's Prayer

Our Father, who art in heaven,
 hallowed be thy Name,
 thy kingdom come,
 thy will be done,
  on earth as it is in heaven.
Give us this day our daily bread.
And forgive us our trespasses,
 as we forgive those
  who trespass against us.
And lead us not into temptation,
 but deliver us from evil.

Our Father in heaven,
 hallowed be your Name,
 your kingdom come,
 your will be done,
  on earth as in heaven.
Give us today our daily bread.
Forgive us our sins
 as we forgive those
  who sin against us.
Save us from the time of trial,
 and deliver us from evil.

The Collect

Visit this place, O Lord, and drive far from it all snares of the
enemy; let your holy angels dwell with us to preserve us in
peace; and let your blessing be upon us always; through Jesus
Christ our Lord. *Amen.*

The almighty and merciful Lord, Father, Son, and Holy Spirit,
bless us and keep us. *Amen.*

Compline

The Officiant begins

The Lord Almighty grant us a peaceful night and a perfect end. *Amen.*

Officiant	Our help is in the Name of the Lord;
People	The maker of heaven and earth.

The Officiant may then say

Let us confess our sins to God.

Silence may be kept.

Officiant and People

Almighty God, our heavenly Father:
We have sinned against you,
through our own fault,
in thought, and word, and deed,
and in what we have left undone.
For the sake of your Son our Lord Jesus Christ,
forgive us all my offenses;
and grant that we may serve you
in newness of life,
to the glory of your Name. *Amen.*

Officiant

May the Almighty God grant us forgiveness of all our sins,
and the grace and comfort of the Holy Spirit. *Amen.*

The Officiant then says
O God, make speed to save us.
People   O Lord, make haste to help us.

Officiant and People
Glory to the Father, and to the Son, and to the Holy Spirit: as it
was in the beginning, is now, and will be for ever. Amen.

Except in Lent, add Alleluia.

*The following Psalm is sung or said. Other suitable selections may be
substituted.*

Psalm 4 *Cum invocarem*

1   Answer me when I call, O God, defender of my cause; *
        you set me free when I am hardpressed;
        have mercy on me and hear my prayer.

2   "You mortals, how long will you dishonor my glory? *
        how long will you worship dumb idols
        and run after false gods?"

3   Know that the LORD does wonders for the faithful; *
        when I call upon the LORD, he will hear me.

4   Tremble, then, and do not sin; *
        speak to your heart in silence upon your bed.

5   Offer the appointed sacrifices *
        and put your trust in the LORD.

6   Many are saying,
        "Oh, that we might see better times!" *
        Lift up the light of your countenance upon us, O LORD.

7   You have put gladness in my heart, *
        more than when grain and wine and oil increase.

8   I lie down in peace; at once I fall asleep; *
        for only you, LORD, make me dwell in safety.

Glory to the Father, and to the Son, and to the Holy Spirit: *
as it was in the beginning, is now, and will be for ever. *Amen.*

Scripture

Others may be chosen.

Be sober, be watchful. Your adversary the devil prowls around like
a roaring lion, seeking someone to devour. Resist him, firm in your
faith. *1 Peter 5:8–9a*

People   Thanks be to God.

A hymn suitable for the evening may be sung.

Then follows

V. Into your hands, O Lord, I commend my spirit;
R. For you have redeemed me, O Lord, O God of truth.
V. Keep us, O Lord, as the apple of your eye;
R. Hide us under the shadow of your wings.

Lord, have mercy.
Christ, have mercy.
Lord, have mercy.

Officiant and People

Our Father, who art in heaven,
  hallowed be thy Name,
  thy kingdom come,
  thy will be done,
    on earth as it is in heaven.
Give us this day our daily bread.
And forgive us our trespasses,
  as we forgive those
    who trespass against us.
And lead us not into temptation,
  but deliver us from evil.
	Our Father in heaven,
	  hallowed be your Name,
	  your kingdom come,
	  your will be done,
	    on earth as in heaven.
	Give us today our daily bread.
	Forgive us our sins
	  as we forgive those
	    who sin against us.
	Save us from the time of trial,
	  and deliver us from evil.

Officiant Lord, hear our prayer;
People And let our cry come to you.
Officiant Let us pray.

The Officiant then says one of the following Collects

Be our light in the darkness, O Lord, and in your great mercy
defend us from all perils and dangers of this night; for the love
of your only Son, our Savior Jesus Christ. *Amen.*

Keep watch, dear Lord, with those who work, or watch, or weep
this night, and give your angels charge over those who sleep.
Tend the sick, Lord Christ; give rest to the weary, bless the dying,
soothe the suffering, pity the afflicted, shield the joyous; and all
for your love's sake. *Amen.*

Prayers of the People

Whatever you ask for in prayer with faith,
you will receive.
    Matthew 21:22

You might recognize the Prayers of the People from Sunday worship. The Prayers of the People are part of every Sunday liturgy and are the moments that join God's Word and God's world together. Praying together is one of the most important responsibilities of people who worship in public.

These prayers for the church, our country, the world, and our own communities can be part of our personal prayer too. We can also include prayers for those who are sick and those who have died.

The prayers here are in the form of a collect (pronounced kol′·ekt)—a prayer that "collects" us into one body to pray. They usually focus on one theme. Every Sunday service has two collects: the collect of purity that begins the service and the collect of the day. You can read these collects on pages 159 to 261 in *The Book of Common Prayer*.

A collect is written like a letter. You address God. You ask for something. You tell God what you're going to do with it. You conclude. Collects can get pretty complicated, so here's a simple formula:

1. Address God using words that call on God, such as "Dear God who loves me," just like in a letter you'd say dear so-and-so. God is so many things. That's why you add words that describe God.
2. Ask God for something such as, "Open my heart."
3. State what you will do with what God gives you such as, "so that I can love other people." *Amen.*

The Prayers of the People cover six areas: the church, the nation, the world, the local community, people who are suffering, and people who have died. So if you're writing the Prayers of the People for a service, make sure you write one for each. Here is one complete set:

1. The church

Holy Spirit, you join us together in a common bond of love and faith in Jesus Christ. Keep all churches focused on God's mission of healing and reconciliation of all people. Give wisdom to those who lead the church: lay leaders, deacons, priests, and bishops. Strengthen all of us to do your work in the world, so that we will be drawn closer to your kingdom here on earth every day. *Amen.*

2. The nation

God of all people and nations, help us to work together for peace and harmony. Help the leaders of our country remember that we are all created in your image, and that in working together we can accomplish so much more. For it is in the combining of our efforts for the good of all humanity that we can all be truly free. *Amen.*

3. The welfare of the world

You tell us to feed the hungry, give drink to the thirsty, welcome the stranger, clothe the naked, care for the sick, and visit the imprisoned. Bless all who provide comfort to those in need. Keep our own eyes open to the opportunities in which we can minister to others. For in the eyes of others, we shall see you. *Amen.*

4. Concerns of your local community

Watch over all who live and work in (*name of your city or town*).
Keep those who protect us safe, including our firefighters and
police officers. Give courage to those who represent us in
government. Provide the skills needed for all who work in our
hospitals and schools. Grant us all compassion to live and work
together so we may make our community a sign of your presence
in the world. *Amen.*

5. The suffering and those in trouble

Heavenly Creator of all, keep watch over those who are in pain
or hurt in any way today. Protect those who find themselves
in trouble or in danger. May your presence comfort them and
give them courage to face their difficulties. For with you, we are
never alone. *Amen.*

6. Those who have died

God, you give us life. You are also with us in death. Hold (*name*)
and all who have died in your arms that they might be at peace.
Comfort us in our sadness. Let us remember (*name*) with joy and
thanksgiving for the time we had together. Give rest to all of us,
for we know that with you there is no sorrow or pain, but life
everlasting. *Amen.*

KINDS OF PRAYER

The prayer of the righteous is powerful and effective.
James 5:16b

Prayer is talking with God; like talking to your best friend. It's easy to talk to someone when you know they love you no matter what. And God loves YOU unconditionally—no strings attached. Sometimes we pray to thank God. Other times we ask for something. There are times when we confess our sins. There are seven principal kinds of prayer used in The Episcopal Church. You might try writing one of each.

Adoration is when we focus our heart and mind on God, simply to enjoy being in the company of God. "God, I love you."

Praise is when we celebrate that God is God and worth our respect and love. "God, how great you are!"

Thanksgiving is offered to God for all the blessings, or good things, we have received in our lives, including whatever brings us closer to God. "God, I thank you for . . ."

Penitence is when we admit we've done wrong. This type of prayer also includes our desire to make things right again, as best as we are able. "God, I confess . . ."

Oblation is when we give ourselves to God, handing over to God who we are and what we are doing. "God, here I am."

Intercession is to pray for others, bringing what they need or desire before God. "God, please help . . ."

Petition is when we bring our own wants and needs to God. "God, help me . . ."

The following prayers from the Bible, *The Book of Common Prayer,* and the hymnals of The Episcopal Church are examples of these seven kinds of prayer. Use them as a framework for saying prayers in your own words.

7. Praise

Holy God
Holy and Mighty
Holy Immortal One
Have mercy upon us.[1]

8. Penitence *(confession)*

Do not be ashamed to confess your sins. Sirach 4:26a

Have mercy on me, O God, according to your loving-kindness;
    in your great compassion blot out my offenses.
Wash me through and through from my wickedness
    and cleanse me from my sin.
For I know my transgressions,
And my sin is ever before me.
Create in me a clean heart, O God,
    and renew a right spirit within me.
Cast me not away from your presence
    and take not your holy Spirit from me.
Give me the joy of your saving help again
    and sustain me with your bountiful Spirit.[2]

---

1. This prayer is known as the *Trisagion* (Greek for "thrice holy")
and is said three times.

2. Psalm 51:1–2; 11–13 (King David's prayer of repentance for cleansing and pardon).

9. Adoration

Worship the Lord in holy splendor. 1 Chronicles 16:29

God of all time,
all seasons of our living,
source of our spark,
protector of our flame,
blazing before our birth,
beyond our dying,
God of all time,
we come to sing your name.

Here in this place,
where others have been building,
we come to claim the legacy of faith,
take, in our turn
the telling of your story,
and, though we tremble,
speak your hope, your truth.[3]

3. God of all time, verses 1 and 2, *Voices Found* (New York: Church Publishing Incorporated, 2003) #86; words: Shirley Erena Murray © 1992 Hope Publishing Company, Carol Stream, IL 60188. All rights reserved. Used with permission.

10. Thanksgiving

Give thanks in all circumstances; for this is the will of God in Christ Jesus for you. 1 Thessalonians 5:18

O God, who created all peoples in your image, we thank you for the wonderful diversity of races and cultures in this world. Enrich our lives by ever-widening circles of fellowship, and show us your presence in those who differ most from us, until our knowledge of your love is made perfect in our love for all your children; through Jesus Christ our Lord. *Amen.*[4]

11. Intercession *(asking for others)*

Moreover, as for me, far be it from me that I should sin against the Lord by ceasing to pray for you. 1 Samuel 12:23

For this reason I bow my knees before the Father, from whom every family in heaven and on earth takes its name. I pray that, according to the riches of his glory, he may grant that you may be strengthened in your inner being with power through his Spirit, and that Christ may dwell in your hearts through faith, as you are being rooted and ground in love. I pray that you may have the power to comprehend, with all the saints, what is the breadth and length and height and depth, and to know the love of Christ that surpasses knowledge, so that you may be filled with all the fullness of God.[5]

---

4. "For the Diversity of Races and Culture," *The Book of Common Prayer,* 840.

5. Ephesians 3:14–19 (the Apostle Paul's prayer for the Ephesians—people from the city of Ephesus, which is in modern-day Turkey).

12. Oblation *(giving to God)*

Then I heard the voice of the Lord saying, "Whom shall I send, and who will go for us?" And I said, "Here am I; send me!" Isaiah 6:8

And here we offer and present unto thee, O Lord, our selves, our souls and our bodies, to be a reasonable, holy, and living sacrifice to thee; humbly beseeching thee that we, and all others who shall be partakers of this Holy Communion, may worthily receive the most precious Body and Blood of thy Son Jesus Christ, be filled with thy grace and heavenly benediction, and made one body with him, that he may dwell in us, and we in him.[6]

13. Petition *(asking for yourself)*

And this is the boldness we have in him, that if we ask anything according to his will, he hears us. 1 John 5:14

Take my life, and let it be consecrated, Lord, to thee;
take my moments and my days, let them flow in ceaseless praise.
Take my hands, and let them move at the impulse of my love;
take my heart, it is thine own; it shall be thy royal throne.

Take my voice, and let me sing always, only, for my King;
take my intellect, and use every power as thou shalt choose.
Take my will, and make it thine; it shall be no longer mine.
Take myself, and I will be ever, only, all for thee.[7]

---

6. A portion of "The Prayer of Consecration" from Rite I, *The Book of Common Prayer*, 336.

7. *The Hymnal 1982* (New York: The Church Pension Fund, 1985) #707, *Hollingside*; words: Frances Ridley Havergal.

PERSONAL PRAYER

Give ear to my prayer, O God;
do not hide yourself from my supplication.
Attend to me, and answer me.
Psalm 55:1–2a

You've probably learned the two special words: "Please" and "Thank you." They're probably what we say most often to God. Before the state basketball finals? *Please!* After winning the state title? *Thank you!* Asking, thanking, and generally talking to God is what we call personal prayer.

Don't worry if you can't seem to find the right words. You're not alone. Paul wrote, "Likewise the Spirit helps us in our weakness; for we do not know how to pray as we ought, but that very Spirit intercedes with sighs too deep for words. And God, who searches the heart, knows what is the mind of the Spirit, because the Spirit intercedes for the saints according to the will of God" (*Romans 8:26–27*). God knows what you need even before you ask.

God's people from the earliest times called on God in times of trouble, joy, sorrow, and searching. Jonah prayed for help while in the belly of a fish (Jonah 2). Hagar pleaded for her son, Ishmael, to not die (Exodus 21:16). The stories of God's people can inspire our own prayers. This ancient practice of praying with the Bible is called *lectio divina*—divine reading.

- *Lectio* (read): choose a passage from the Bible and read it very slowly several times. Try reading it aloud, even if you are alone.

- *Meditatio* (meditate): listen for the word that captures your attention. Say it a few times to hear what the word might be saying. Follow your imagination.

- *Oratio* (pray): tell God what you heard from the passage and listen for what God may be calling you to do.

- *Contemplatio* (contemplate): in silence let yourself feel the love of God.

If you're a little nervous about praying, think of it like talking to a new friend. At first you might not know what to say. As you get to know one another, however, talking just comes naturally. The same is true for talking to God. The more you pray, the more you and God will get to know one another.

The prayers that follow about faith, friends, family, school, major events, and more can give you a start on the conversation. You'll see a Bible verse before each prayer. If the prayer doesn't really fit what you want to say, you might read the Bible verse carefully, think of what you want to pray, and see what words come to mind. You know best what is on your heart. Actually, God knows even before you know. Sometimes just being silent will help you hear what God hears, and what God is saying to you.

Faith

O come, let us sing to the Lord;
let us make a joyful noise to the rock of our salvation!
Let us come into his presence with thanksgiving.
    Psalm 95:1

14. Feeling close to God

The kingdom of God is among you. Luke 17:21

I feel the sunshine on my face
    and the warmth of your love that surrounds me.
The beating of my heart and the expansion of my lungs
    remind me of the life within me.
With you, God, I live, and move, and have my being.

In the stillness of my being and the movement of my body,
    I am amazed at how alive I am.
My thoughts and memories connect my past and my present,
    as I anticipate the future.
With you, God, I live, and move, and have my being.

Your hand is always on my shoulder.
With you, God, I live, and move, and have my being.

15. Feeling far away from God

My soul yearns for you in the night, my spirit within me earnestly seeks you. Isaiah 26:9a

My heart yearns for you, oh God,
you find me where I am.

You are far away.
I cannot hear you.
I cannot see the path before me.
I feel alone.

Draw me near to you.
Tune my ears to your voice.
Awaken my taste to your goodness.
Embrace me with your warmth.
Shed light before me.

My heart yearns for you, oh God,
you find me where I am.[8]

---

8. From the song "My Heart Yearns for You" by Fran McKendree. Used with permission.

16. Confirmation

In him you also, when you had heard the word of truth, the gospel of your salvation, and had believed in him, were marked with the seal of the promised Holy Spirit. Ephesians 1:13

God, I am ready.
Jesus, I want to follow you.
Spirit, stay with me.

Be present with me today as I reaffirm my baptismal promises. Thank you for those who have helped me prepare for this day, especially *(names)*. Send your Holy Spirit upon me. Give me the strength to be the person you created me to be, to love and serve you to the best of my ability, today and in all the days to come. *Amen.*

17. Before receiving communion

While they were eating, he took a loaf of bread, and after blessing it he said, "Take; this is my body." Then he took a cup, and after giving thanks he gave it to them, and all of them drank from it. He said to them, "This is my blood of the covenant, which is poured out for many." Mark 14:22–24

Be present, be present, Jesus, as you were present with your disciples, and be known to me in the breaking of the bread.

18. Discipleship

Go therefore and make disciples of all nations, baptizing them
in the name of the Father and of the Son and of the Holy Spirit.
Matthew 28:19

I want to walk as a child of the Light.
I want to follow Jesus.
God set the stars to give light to the world.
The star of my life is Jesus.

In him there is no darkness at all.
The night and the day are both alike.
The Lamb is the light of the city of God.
Shine in my heart, Lord Jesus.

I want to see the brightness of God.
I want to look at Jesus.
Clear sun of righteousness, shine on my path,
and show me the way to the Father.

I'm looking for the coming of Christ.
I want to be with Jesus.
When we have run with patience the race,
we shall know the joy of Jesus.[9]

---

9. *The Hymnal 1982* #490 *Houston*; words: Kathleen Thomerson.

19. Reading the Bible

Keep these words that I am commanding you today in your heart.
Deuteronomy 6:6

God, whose Word has broken into the world,
    you are always with me
    to hear what I have to say.
Quiet my mind so that I can
    hear your Holy Word.

Prepare my heart to hear our stories
    of call and return,
    failure and mercy,
    hurt and healing,
    peril and safety.

Stories of when we have turned away.
Stories of your steadfast love.

And more than hearing your Word,
Write them on my heart.
Give me the grace to know and live them.

Through the Day

But do not ignore this one fact, beloved,
that with the Lord one day is like a thousand years,
and a thousand years are like one day.
> *2 Peter 3:8*

Days of the Week

20. Sunday

Today is the day I go to church to bless you. It's the day we gather to receive your blessings. It's the day we hear your word and come to your table. It's the day we are fed so we can go out into the world on Monday to live as you would have us live. Thank you for this day.

21. Monday

A new week has begun when everything can become new again. Give me strength at home, at school, and at work to live in the life of your son, Jesus Christ, so that I can be a part of your new creation. (*Based on 2 Corinthians 5:17*)

22. Tuesday

Sometimes my weekly path takes unexpected turns. Unexpected challenges. Surprising joys. Give me strength, wisdom, and courage to respond with humility to today's challenges. Make my heart light to delight in joy. Guide me through this week's twists and turns.

23. Wednesday

Thank you for the week so far. What has passed is past. The future is yet to be. Today is what is now. Help me to welcome this day and live this moment. Help me to seek the light of Christ, your Son, in my friends, my teachers, and my family. Help me to hold onto this moment. This day.

24. Thursday

God who makes our days long and our nights short, help me to pursue righteousness, godliness, faith, love, endurance, and gentleness. I want to fight the good fight of the faith and take hold of the eternal life, to which I am called. Strengthen me to keep your commandments without spot or blame and be part of your new creation. To you be honor and everlasting power. (*Based on 1 Timothy 6:11–16*)

25. Friday

God, who set the sun and the moon in the sky, making day and night, we are at the closing of the week. Thank you for giving us your only Son who walked on the earth as I have this week. Through its ups and its downs. Thank you for bringing us to our new life in Christ. (*Based on Genesis 1:16–17*)

26. Saturday

God who created the heavens and the earth, when you finished your work, you rested, and blessed creation. Quiet my mind, quiet my body, and quiet my soul from all the busyness of my week so that I, too, can rest and return the blessings of my week to you. (*Based on Genesis 2:1–3*)

27. Waking up

Awake, my soul!
Awake, O harp and lyre!
I will awake the dawn. Psalm 57:8

The night is over.
The day has dawned.

Awaken my spirit
to the wonder and joy
of your creation.
Stir within me a love
for those I will meet.

The night is over.
The morning has come.
Rise up with me, Lord Jesus.

28. Grace at meals

Give us grateful hearts, our Father, for all your mercies, and make us mindful of the needs of others; through Jesus Christ our Lord. *Amen.*[10]

29. Table blessing

Thank you for the meal in front of us.
A meal that feeds our bodies,
    our minds, and our spirits.
Thank you for the hands that prepared it.
Thank you for the farmers who grew the vegetables and fruits,
    raised the cows, chickens, and pigs,
    caught the fish.
Thank you for the workers who gathered the vegetables,
    picked the fruit,
    fed the livestock.
Thank you for the meal in front of us.
May it strengthen our bodies and our minds
so that our actions as well as our words
give thanks to you.

---

10. *The Book of Common Prayer*, 835.

30. Leaving for the day

The LORD will keep your going out and your coming in from this time on and forevermore. Psalm 121:8

God who traces my coming in and my going out,
give me confidence and hope.
Keep me safe from darkness.
Bless those who cross my path.
Help me see your light in all people.

31. Returning from the day

In returning and rest you shall be saved; in quietness and in trust shall be your strength. Isaiah 30:15

It's the end of the day.
Where did it go?
What did I get done?
Does it matter?
You said to Moses,
"Tell them 'I AM' sent you."
Am I loved because of
what I do? Or
because I am?
Sometimes I just want to be.
To be loved because
I am.

32. The end of the day

O gracious Light,
pure brightness of the everliving Father in heaven,
O Jesus Christ, holy and blessed!

Now as we come to the setting of the sun,
and our eyes behold the vesper light,
We sing your praises, O God: Father, Son, and Holy Spirit.

You are worthy at all times to be praised by happy voices,
O Son of God, O Giver of Life,
and to be glorified through all the worlds.[11]

33. Going to bed

Guide us waking, and guard us sleeping;
that awake we may watch with Christ,
and asleep we may rest in peace.[12]

---

11. O gracious light (*Phos Hilaron*—Greek for "light of glory") can be found in Evening Prayer II, *The Book of Common Prayer*, 118.

12. Antiphon for the *Song of Simeon* in Compline, *The Book of Common Prayer*, 134.

Through the Year

You are observing special days, and months, and seasons, and years.
    Galatians 4:10

We keep track of time in many ways. During the day it's by the minute and hour. Over the year it's by the month. We also measure time with seasons—winter, spring, summer, and fall for some and the dry season and the rainy season for others. Maybe you keep track of season with sports—the lacrosse and field hockey seasons. We keep time based on what's important in our lives.

The Christian Church orders its year with the liturgical calendar, which chronicles the story of Jesus' life and how the first Christians practiced their faith. The word "liturgical" comes from the Greek word *leitourgia*, meaning "the work of the people." The liturgical calendar connects Jesus' life with ours.

The liturgical calendar grew out of the need of the early church to instruct candidates for baptism on the important stories and teachings of the church. These stories provided the foundation for the newly baptized and all members of the church in their new life together. It continues to order our common life in Christ.

The church year is marked by weeks that begin with Sunday, the day that Jesus rose from the dead. These weeks are organized into seasons. The first is Advent, when we prepare, with John the Baptist, to make way for Jesus. Advent doesn't begin in January as the common calendar does. It begins four Sundays before Christmas Day. Each of the seasons of the church year helps us to remember that we are God's people, called to follow the way of Christ. The following are the seven seasons of the liturgical year:

Advent—We recall how our people waited for the coming of the Messiah, Jesus. We express our dreams and hopes for the future along with our vision of a life with Christ.

Christmas—We recall the birth of Jesus in Bethlehem and celebrate times of new birth in our own lives.

Epiphany—We remember the many ways Jesus revealed himself to the world. We realize our responsibility to show Christ's love and power to the world.

Lent—Following the example of Jesus' forty days in the wilderness and his temptations, we look at our temptations and failures as individuals and society and prepare to reaffirm our baptismal promises to God. Part of Lent is *Holy Week* when we dramatize the last week of Jesus' life, including his arrest, trial, and crucifixion. We walk with Jesus, the disciples, and generations of pilgrims on the road to the cross.

Easter—We proclaim Jesus' resurrection. During these seven weeks we celebrate God's gift of grace and how God continues to touch our lives today with joy and wonder.

The Day of Pentecost—On this day the church dramatizes in word, action, and symbol the apostles' receiving the gift of the Holy Spirit. We celebrate the Holy Spirit who comes to us through the sacraments and our experiences of power and inspiration.

The Season after Pentecost—Also called "ordinary time," during this season we recognize God in the ordinary movements of our lives as well as in the times of intense emotions and celebrations.

The following prayers are offered to help you keep time in God's way. As we tell and retell the story of Jesus and of the people of God over many years, they become more familiar and powerful. They become woven into the "seasons" of our own lives—waiting, celebrating, noticing Jesus' face around us, and proclaiming good news. Think of the liturgical seasons as "seasons of the soul."

34. Advent

The people who walked in darkness have seen a great light; those who lived in a land of darkness—on them light has shined. Isaiah 9:2b

Thank you for this time of waiting
    to be still amid life's busyness
    to hear your call amid life's noise
    to prepare a way in this world for you.

Thank you for this time of preparing
    to clear away the clutter
    to make room in my crammed life
    to receive the light of Christ that awakens me.

Thank you for this time of awakening
    to notice that you are with us
    to hear your voice in the night
    calling us to bring your light to people.

Thank you for your light in the world.
I want to walk as a child of your light.

35. Christmas

And she gave birth to her firstborn son and wrapped him in bands of cloth, and laid him in a manger, because there was no place for them in the inn. Luke 2:7

Christ is born!
Praises to our Creator God, who became flesh for us most fully
    in Jesus, the Incarnate Word
To become one of us, human, yet divine.

Christ is born!
My heart sings that the time of waiting is over.
The light has overcome the darkness as
    the true gift from God has arrived.

Christ is born!
Praises to our Creator God, who is as close as the love that binds
    us, one to another,
Filling us with awe and wonder at such miracles.

Christ is born!
Help us to live the joy of Jesus' birth this and every day,
    knowing that the Spirit of Christ dwells in us
        guiding us to be his witnesses in all that we say and do
            throughout the year.

Christ is born!

36. Epiphany

Arise, shine, for your light has come, and the glory of the LORD *has risen upon you. Nations shall come to your light, and kings to the brightness of your dawn. Isaiah 60:1, 3*

Brightest and best of the stars of the morning,[13]
Help us remember that Jesus is the light in the darkness.

Brightest and best of the stars of the morning,
Keep our eyes focused on each new day.

Brightest and best of the stars of the morning,
Lead us out into the world.

---

13. This is the first line of the poem by Reginald Heber which is used in two Epiphany hymns: *Morning Star* #117 and *Star in the East* #118.

37. Lent

Yes even now, says the LORD, return to me with all your heart, with fasting, with weeping, and with mourning; rend your hearts and not your clothing. Return to the LORD, your God, for he is gracious and merciful, slow to anger, and abounding in steadfast love, and relents from punishing. Joel 2:12–13

Forgiving God, stay with me
    as I walk through Lent
    for these next forty days.

Help me to learn more about myself
    during this time you have given me for
    prayer and discernment.

Open my eyes as I walk with Jesus at my side,
    so that I can see any
    new path you want me to follow.

Open my ears to what you are saying
    when I read and
    study the Bible.

More than anything, know that I'm sorry
    to have forgotten you this past year.
    I seek to return to you more fully in the coming days.

This I pray in the name of
    my guide,
    Your Son, Jesus.

38. Easter

He is not here, for he has been raised, as he said. Matthew 28:6a

Alleluia! You have risen! Alleluia!

It is a mystery.
>You were nailed on a cross.
>You died.
>They put you in a tomb and sealed the door.

It is a mystery.
>The tomb is now empty.
>You are alive.
>Death is nothing to you.

It is a mystery.
>You have opened a door for me.
>Continue to show me the way to God.
>Help me remember the joy of this day.

Alleluia! You have risen. Alleluia!

39. The Day of Pentecost

Many signs and wonders were done among the people through the apostles. Acts 5:12a

Spirit God,
Pour your gifts upon me.
Let your Spirit speak through me.

Your Story is too precious to keep to myself.
Help me to be a disciple,
    sharing the joy I have
    to be your child
    and a friend of Jesus'.

Let my excitement spread like the wind,
    just as fire, wind, and spirit cannot be contained.
I am bursting at the seams
    to tell your story.

40. Season after Pentecost

As for mortals, their days are like grass;
they flourish like a flower of the field. Psalm 103:15

The days are getting longer.
Keep your Spirit in my heart and mind
    during this growing season.
Be with me as I finish the school year,
    participate in summer activities,
    enjoy the gift of summer turning into fall.

Help me recognize your works in all that I do
    at work,
    at rest,
    and at play,
so that I can give thanks for all you provide,
    even without my even asking.

41. Birthdays

You have granted me life and steadfast love, and your care has preserved my spirit. Job 10:12

God, who gave me life and steadfast love,
You have been my friend and companion for another year.
Through sadness and joy. In losses and victories.
In ordinary days and extraordinary days.

When I fell short, you picked me up.
When I did well, you celebrated.
When I cried, you wiped my tears.
When I shouted for joy, you shouted with me.
When I was lonely, you stayed with me.
When I was hurt, you held me more tightly.

Good-bye to another year.
Hello to a new one.

God, who gave me life and steadfast love,
be with me, my friend and companion,
again this coming year.

42. Thanksgiving Day

He has told you, O mortal, what is good; and what does the LORD *require of you but to do justice, and to love kindness, and to walk humbly with your God? Micah 6:8*

God of abundance,
> In a world where some do not have enough,
> Make us brave to share out of our own richness.

God of justice,
> In a world where some have far more than others,
> Make us bold to provide for all people.

God of mercy,
> In a world broken with a desire for more,
> Forgive us for taking the greater portions.

Thanks and praise to you,
> God of abundance
> God of justice
> God of mercy.

Be with us and all people this day.

43. For a youth event

Lift up your heads, O gates!
and be lifted up, O ancient doors!
that the King of glory may come in. Psalm 24:7

God our King of glory, we come together in your name,
  lifting our heads and opening the doors to you.
Come in and be with us during this time
  as we learn, work, pray, worship, and play together.

Unlock our hearts to welcome one another.
Knit us into one community.
Fill our voices to sing your praise.

Bless the youth. Bless the leaders.
Bless all those who prepared this event.
Bless the church that keeps us.

Set a path of goodness before us.
Place a lamp at our feet to keep us on your way.
Bring us to our journey's end in safety.

And in all things, may what we do witness to your glory.

Self

Let your adornment be the inner self with
the lasting beauty of a gentle and quiet spirit,
which is very precious in God's sight.
    1 Peter 3:4

44. Accepting myself

For it was you who formed my inward parts;
you knit me together in my mother's womb. Psalm 139:13

God of all people and all creation,
You made me. You know me.
You love each and every part of me:
every cell, every organ, every single hair.
I am beautiful in your sight.
Hold me fast when others do not accept me,
Fill me with your love when I do not accept myself.
Strengthen my spirit.
Fill my heart with celebration.
Endure with me until that time when
others see that I am beautiful,
others accept me for who I am.
All of me.

45. Courage

I took courage, for the hand of the Lord my God was upon me.
Ezra 7:28b

Give me the courage to face *(name the danger or difficulty).*
Help me to overcome fear that should not overtake me.
Help me to listen to fear that cautions me rightly.
Give me the strength to do what I have to do.
Help me to be brave, knowing that your hand is upon me.
And if today is not the day to face this,
Give me the courage to try again tomorrow.

46. Anger

For a fire is kindled by my anger, and burns to the depths of Sheol.
Deuteronomy 32:22a

Anger burns inside me.
    The heat rises within me.
It is hard to hold my temper.
    Words fly out of my mouth.

I'm so angry toward (*name*) I can't stand it.
    It's consuming me.
I am so mad at (*name*).
    I can't see beyond my rage.

Lord, I know it's okay to be angry.
    You get angry too.
Help me take this fire within me,
    and use it to do what's right, not for revenge.

47. Joy

We are writing these things so that our joy may be complete.
1 John 1:4

Everything in my life is coming together.
I can't stop smiling.
I want to sing and dance—and I don't care who sees me!
Thank you God for (*name what is giving you joy*).

48. Anxiety

Cast all your anxiety on him, because he cares for you. 1 Peter 5:7

Calm me.
Release everything that's making me anxious,
    especially (*name whatever is pressing in upon you*).
Fill every cell of my body with your presence.
Help me feel your love everywhere:
    in my body, in my brain, and in my soul.
Hold me in your arms
    so I can let this tension go.

Your love is stronger than anything.

49. Confidence

Do not, therefore, abandon that confidence of yours; it brings a great reward. Hebrews 10:35

Christ within me, you are my strength.
Christ in front of me, you light the way.
Christ behind me, you guide my actions.
Christ to the right of me, you are my companion.
Christ to the left of me, a companion twice.
Christ beneath me, you ground me.
Christ above me, you lift my eyes to you.

Christ all around, I go forward with confidence.
With you, I can do it.

50. Body image

I praise you, for I am fearfully and wonderfully made.
Wonderful are your works. Psalm 139:14

Creator God, you made all things.
You made us in your image and blessed us.

Help me to see that you bless me too.
Bless my hand and foot,
    finger and toe,
    chest and head,
    eyes and hair,
    height and weight.
You made every part of me
    and I am beautiful.

Help me turn away from things and people
    that tell me I'm ugly,
    that I don't fit in.

I am awesome and wonderfully made.
Help me believe this.

51. Boredom

In the morning sow your seed, and at evening do not let your hands be idle; for you do not know which will prosper, this or that, or whether both alike will be good. Ecclesiastes 11:6

My heart is restless, I have nothing to do.

I'm bored.

Same thing every day.
> Wake up. Go to school. Go to class.
> Do homework. Play video games.
> Eat. Go to sleep.
> And the next day all over again.
It's boring. What's the point?

God, give me something to do.
> Something I can be excited about.
> Something that matters.
> A new adventure.

Help me to see my purpose in life.

My heart is restless, let me rest in you.[14]

---

14. Based on the words of St. Augustine of Hippo (CE 354–430).

52. Broken trust

Your trusted friends have seduced you and have overcome you; Now that your feet are stuck in the mud, they desert you. Jeremiah 38:22b

My heart is breaking.
I trusted (name) to (action: keep a secret, help me, etc.)
    and they broke their promise.
They let me down. They hurt me. They deserted me.
I know no one is perfect.
But this really hurt.

Can I trust anyone again?
I can trust you. You will never desert me.

When it's right, help me to trust again.
My trust is always with you.

53. Car accident

How often have I desired to gather your children together as a hen gathers her brood under her wings. Luke 13:34b

God, my comforter, I've been in a car accident and I'm still shaking. Thank you for being with me during and after the accident. It could have been a lot worse. Thank you for everyone who helped me since the accident, especially (name friends, family members, law enforcement officers, etc). Heal my body, mind, and spirit. Help me to be careful and confident when I drive again. Take me under your wings and keep me safe.

54. Healing

Come to me, all you that are weary and are carrying heavy burdens, and I will give you rest. Matthew 11:28

O God, you care for your creation with great tenderness.
In the midst of the greatest pain, you offer hope.
Help me (*or name of person*),
    my (*his/her*) spirit seems to be lost
    and soul is in despair.
Heal my (*or name of person*) wounds
    and be with those who care for me (*him/her*).
Let me (*him/her*) feel your pure love.
Let me (*him/her*) believe in the miracle of rebirth
    so that I (*he/she*) can experience now
    a small taste of the happiness
    I hope to know in eternity.[15]

55. Fear

I hereby command you: Be strong and courageous; do not be frightened or dismayed, for the LORD your God is with you wherever you go. Joshua 1:9

Lord, I am afraid.
My fear has trapped and consumed me.
Help me to be strong and courageous.
Allow me to let go of what frightens and troubles me.
Give me strength to confront my fears and ask others for help.
There isn't anything we can't handle together.

---

15. Based on a prayer by Dimma, a seventh-century Irish monk.

56. Disappointment

Endurance produces character, and character produces hope, and hope does not disappoint us, because God's love has been poured into our hearts through the Holy Spirit that has been given to us. Romans 5:4–5

Sadness, frustration, emptiness.
My heart is breaking.
What I hoped for didn't happen.
Nothing turned out the way I wished it would.
I feel so alone and let down.
What a waste, what a disappointment.
Help me move on.
Fill my heart so I can smile again.

57. Patience

Be patient, therefore, beloved, until the coming of the LORD. The farmer waits for the precious crop from the earth, being patient with it until it receives the early and the late rains. James 5:7

When will this (*day, class, project, car ride, etc.*) end?
I get so frustrated, impatient, and angry
    when things don't go right.
Please give me the patience to enjoy each minute of each day,
    the ability to take a deep breath and close my eyes, and
    the calmness to know that (*name the issue*) will work out.
All in your time, God. All in your time.

58. Depression

O my God, I cry by day, but you do not answer;
and by night, but find no rest. Psalm 22:2

I'm tired.
I don't feel like doing anything.
I've got no energy.
I want to go to sleep.
I'm sad.
I feel like crying all the time.

Wake me up.
Be with me.
I need help.
Give me strength
to tell someone
I need help.

59. Envy

Do not be conformed to this world, but be transformed by the renewing of your minds, so that you may discern what is the will of God—what is good and acceptable and perfect. Romans 12:2

Everyone else seems to
    wear the trendy clothes,
    get the newest things,
    look better than I do.
More and better. It seems endless.
Take this envy from me.

Give me strength to know
    I do not need to conform to the world.
    I am loved by you, whoever I am.

Thank you for giving me what I have.
Thank you for loving me.
Your love is more than enough.

60. Forgiveness

If we say that we have no sin, we deceive ourselves, and the truth is not in us. If we confess our sins, he who is faithful and just will forgive us our sins and cleanse us from all unrighteousness. 1 John 1:8–10

Faithful God, your love is greater than I can imagine.
I have hurt others—
    by what I have done
    and what I have not done,
    by what I have said
    and what I have not said.
I have (*name particular actions and words*).
You forgive me even before I've done something wrong—
    not so that I will hurt others,
    but so that when I do,
    I can turn around
    and come back to you.
I have sinned and I am sorry.
Forgive me.

61. Being nervous

Strengthen the weak hands,
and make firm the feeble knees. Isaiah 35:3

God of strength and might,
My blood has run right out of my body.
At least that's what it feels like.
I'm not sure I'm ready.
Can I do this?

God of strength and might,
Be with me as I try.

62. Guilt

Take words with you and return to the LORD; say to him, "Take away
all guilt; accept that which is good, and we will offer the fruit of our
lips." Hosea 14:2

My heart is heavy.
My thoughts are troubled.
I feel so bad for what I have said (*or done*).
God, please forgive me.
Take this burden away from me.
Ease my guilt.
Give me strength to make amends
to those whom I have hurt.
Including myself and you, O God.

63. Kindness

A new heart I will give you, and a new spirit I will put within you; and I will remove from your body the heart of stone and give you a heart of flesh. Ezekiel 36:26

Take my heart of stone
    and give me a new heart.
A heart to love you,
A heart to love others.
Loving people who
    look different,
    have a different skin color,
    wear different clothes,
    talk differently than I.
Give me a new heart to love.
Give me a new heart, a heart of flesh.

64. Trust

Trust in the LORD forever, for in the Lord God you have an everlasting rock. Isaiah 26:4

You are my rock.
You are solid.
I trust you to protect me.
I am in your hands.
My hope is in you and your steadfast love.
Hear me.
I am unsteady.
I am unsure.
I trust you.

65. Loneliness

The hour is coming, indeed it has come, when you will be scattered, each one to his home, and you will leave me alone. Yet I am not alone because the Father is with me. John 16:32

Jesus, I feel so alone.
I sit at school
    and the world seems to
    pass me by.
I lay on my bed
    and am surrounded
    by silence.
Jesus, I feel invisible.
Everyone seems busy
    and having so much fun.
Everyone has someone
    to talk to and be with.
Jesus, I feel so alone.
Stay with me.
Wrap your love around me.
Be with me so I'm not so lonely.

66. What is love?

And this is my prayer, that your love may overflow more and more with knowledge and full insight to help you determine what is best. Philippians 1:9–10

What's love, really? I mean *really?*
God is love. Love is patient. Love is kind.
Love means never having to say you're sorry. All you need is love.
Love makes the world go 'round. Love is blind.
Is that what love is?

What's love, really? I mean *really?*
My (*parent/caretaker*) says, "I love you,"
     but doesn't always show it.
(*Name*) said, "I love you,"
     but broke up with me.
Jesus says to love others, but
     we always seem to be at war.
Is that what love is?

What's love, really?
When someone asks how I am and means it.
When my pet (*name*) is happy to see me.
When God forgives me after I screw up.
Giving a hug to someone who needs it.
Listening to someone who is hurt or lonely.
Helping others when they need it.
That's what love is.

Thank you God for loving me.
So I can show what love really is. *Really.*

67. Making decisions

Wisdom is radiant and unfading, and she is easily discerned by those who love her, and is found by those who seek her. Wisdom 6:12

God, making decisions isn't easy.
You say that wisdom shines and never fades.
That if I love wisdom, I'll see her,
    if I seek wisdom, I'll find her.
That wisdom is right here, with me,
    ready to be found.
That if I look early,
    I'll know soon enough.
Help me to see the possibilities
    with a clear head,
    with love in my heart.
Help me to wait until I'm ready to choose.
Give me faith to trust you and myself.

Wisdom is sitting right here with me.
I'm looking right at her. She's shining.
And she's looking right back at me.
Thank you for giving me wisdom.

68. Suicide (thinking about)

Let my prayer come before you; incline your ear to my cry. For my soul is full of troubles, and my life draws near to Sheol. Psalm 88:2–3

I'm empty and I don't feel like living anymore.
I'm in more pain than I can bear right now.
I'm tired. Take all this away from me.
These feelings I have are overwhelming.
I don't know what to do.
Am I worth anything?

God, you say you know me and love me.
Show me your love.
Help me wait another day.
Help me live another day.
I don't know what to do.
Am I worth anything?

Give me the strength to call a friend.
Give me some time to reach out.
Just as you are here to listen,
I know people care.
I don't know what to do.
Am I worth anything?

Take my emptiness upon you.
Bear my burden.
I am worth everything.
Help me to see the goodness in myself
    that I am loved.
    that I am worthy of living.

69. Tired

Come to me, all you that are weary and are carrying heavy burdens,
and I will give you rest. For my yoke is easy, and my burden is light.
Matthew 11:28, 30

I'm tired of it all.
I'm tired of people turning their backs on me.
I'm tired of not being included.
I'm tired of studying and taking exams.
I'm tired of having to please other people.
I'm tired of being angry at everyone and everything.
Take my frustration, my loneliness, my trouble, and my anger.
Make my burden light.
I come to you for rest.

70. Worry

Do not worry about anything, but in everything by prayer and
supplication with thanksgiving let your requests be made known
to God. Philippians 4:6

Let nothing disturb you,
    nothing affright you;
All things are passing,
    God never changes.
Patience attains
    all that it strives for;
Who possesses God
    finds nothing lacking:
God alone suffices.[16]

---

16. Teresa of Avila (CE 1515–1582).

71. Waiting

I wait for the LORD, my soul waits,
and in his word I hope;
my soul waits for the LORD
more than those who watch for the morning,
more than those who watch for the morning. Psalm 130:5–6

Time passes so slowly.
God, why is this taking so long?

Hurry, hurry, hurry.
Then
    wait,
        wait,
            wait.

Jesus, help me remember,
    that time is something that cannot be caught
    and God's time is not my time.

Holy Spirit, settle me down,
    open my heart
    and fill it with your love.

Wait with me.

Milestones

A highway shall be there,
and it shall be called the Holy Way.
        Isaiah 35:8a

72. Earning a driver's license *(or learner's permit)*

The LORD went in front of them in a pillar of cloud by day, to lead them along the way, and in a pillar of fire by night, to give them light, so that they might travel by day and by night. Exodus 13:21

God, my companion on all journeys,
I have been given the gift of driving.
I have more independence
and new responsibilities.
New possibilities lie ahead.

Give me wisdom
    to make good decisions while driving.
Give me patience
    with other drivers when I'm on the road.
Help me concentrate and not be distracted
    when I'm behind the wheel.

Guard those who are in my car and
    everyone on the road against all danger.
Guide my driving by day and by night.

Keep us safe from injury.
Help me to use the gift of driving wisely.

Thank you, God, for this new journey.

73. Growing into a woman (or man)

. . . the whole body, nourished and held together by its ligaments and sinews, grows with growth that is from God. Colossians 2:19b

Dear God, you created me a woman (*man*) in your image.
A woman (*man*) with the power to create.
The power to discover new ideas.
The power to make new friends.
The power to welcome those who are different.
The power to see new ways to care for the world.
The power to love you more each day.
The power to create new life.

I stand among women (*men*) who have come before.
I stand among women (*men*) who are with us today.
Prophets, martyrs, teachers, protectors, healers, saints.
Help me listen to and follow the wisdom of their lives.
Help me grow into the person you made me to be,
Bless them and bless me.

74. Leaving home

Now the LORD said to Abram, "Go from your country and your kindred and your father's house to the land that I will show you."
Genesis 12:1

God of Abraham and Sarah,
Isaac and Rebekah, Jacob and Leah and Rachel,
you call us to new and sometimes
unknown places with the promise of
a full life through your grace and mercy.

Now I am leaving home
for a new place.

Empower my body, mind, and spirit
to receive this new journey
with a spirit of anticipation and delight.

Take away all my fear of the unknown,
for whatever lies ahead, you will be with me.

Sharpen my ears to hear your call.
Clear my eyes to see your path.
Strengthen my hands to do your service.

Protect me from the perils of this world.
Grant me wisdom to make good choices.
Fortify my faith to take risks to do your work.

As I leave this familiar place,
help me continue to grow
in love and service to you.

75. A significant birthday

And Jesus increased in wisdom and in years, and in divine and human favor. Luke 2:52

God, our creator, redeemer, and sanctifier,
You formed me as I am—wonderfully made.
You have conquered death so I can have life.
You make my life holy.

Thank you for the many blessings in my life.
Thank you for the people who love and guide me.
Thank you for experiences that shape me into who I am today.

Give me strength to hold onto those that
    will help me grow in your favor.
Give me courage to let go of those that will hold me back.
Grant me an open heart to embrace new friends,
    new places, and new experiences.

Be with me as I begin new adventures in the coming years,
    being made holy by your grace and favor.

76. Graduation

I have fought the good fight, I have finished the race, I have kept the faith. 2 Timothy 4:7

God of wisdom,
    bless me this day as I cross into a new part of my life.
I have studied and succeeded.
It wasn't always easy, but I have done it!
With your teachings as my guide,
    and the knowledge I have gained at *(name of school)*,
    watch over me as I begin a new chapter in my life.
Walk by my side today,
    and all the days to come.

77. Voting

Hear what the LORD says: Rise, plead your case before the mountains, and let the hills hear your voice. Micah 6:1

Holy Spirit, I have been given a great responsibility this day. Help me to discern the right choice that has been put before me. Be with me as I cast my ballot. May those who are elected respond justly to the trust people have put in them. No matter the outcome of this election, may we all work together for the good of everyone. *Amen.*

Friends and Family

Jonathan said to David, "Go in peace, since both of us have sworn in the name of the Lord, saying, 'The Lord shall be between me and you, and between my descendants and your descendants, forever.'"
1 Samuel 20:42

78. Blessing a friendship

Faithful friends are a sturdy shelter:
whoever finds one has found a treasure. Sirach 6:14

God, you are a friend to all people.
Bless my friendship with (*name*).
I treasure our friendship.

When we play, be happy with us.
When we stand with one another, strengthen us.

When we disagree, help us listen to one another.
When our friendship begins to fall apart, mend us back together.

We love each other.
May we shine your love for everyone.

Being friends means we're not alone.
Help us share our friendship so that others are not alone.

God, bless our friendship.

79. Blessing a family

So then you are no longer strangers and aliens, but you are citizens
with the saints and also members of the household of God.
Ephesians 2:19a

Bless my family, near and far.
A family is created in many ways:
    sometimes by DNA,
    sometimes by sharing experiences,
    sometimes by choosing each other.

Help us to walk together in the light of God's blessing.
Help us to love one another as Christ loves us.
Help us to see Christ in each other.
Help us to forgive each other with Christ's pardon.

Help us to share all that you give us:
    our hopes and dreams, fears and joys,
    sorrow and disappointments.

May our family grow in grace and truth
to live out the blessings you give us.
Whether we are connected through:
    DNA,
    experience,
    or choice.
Bless us.

80. Blessing a home

As for me and my household, we will serve the LORD. *Joshua 24:15b*

God, you dwell with us.
Bless this place we call home.
Bless the room where we prepare meals and eat.
Bless the places where we sleep as well as rest.
Bless where we watch TV, play games, and do homework.
Bless every floor, wall, and ceiling.
Bless every nook and cranny.

Bless those who find shelter.
Bless those who are comforted.
Bless those who share friendship.
Bless all those who I call family.

Give us compassionate hearts
to open our home to those
    who need shelter here,
    who need comfort here.
Bless the guests who come.
In all things may this household serve you.

81. Blessing a pet

God made the wild animals of the earth of every kind, and the cattle of every kind, and everything that creeps upon the ground of every kind. And God saw that it was good. Genesis 1:25

Creator God, you made everything.
Scaly. Furry. Spiny. Feathery.
Hissing. Barking. Meowing. Chirping.
You made us all, different and beautiful.

Thank you particularly for (*name of pet*).
(*She/he*) is loyal and loves me.
(*She/he*) is my companion.
(*She/he*) makes me laugh.
(*She/he*) consoles me.

Thank you for (*name of pet*).
Protect (*her/him*) from danger.
Keep (*her/him*) healthy.
Be with (*her/him*) when I am away.

Bless (*name of pet*).
And bless our friendship.

82. For a family member *(or friend)* deployed in the military

The LORD bless you and keep you; the LORD make his face to shine upon you, and be gracious to you; the LORD lift up his countenance upon you, and give you peace. Numbers 6:24–26

With hope and fear in my heart,
> be with *(name of friend or loved one)*
> as *(he/she)* leaves to serve our country.

Guide and keep *(him/her)* safe.
Calm my anxiety and fears
> as *(he/she)* departs to places that may be dangerous.

May *(he/she)* quickly come back home,
> where I wait,
> knowing that you watch over us all.

83. Going on a trip

You, O LORD, will protect us. Psalm 12:7a

Everlasting God, be with us as we begin this trip. Bless our time together. May our conversations bubble with laughter. May we greet new adventures with a joyful spirit. Smooth our rough edges so that when we are tired, bothered, or disagree, we have space to be calm. Guide us in safety along our way and grant us a safe return. In all things, remind us that we are yours wherever we go. *Amen.*

84. Seeking to be understood

One who spares words is knowledgeable;
one who is cool in spirit
has understanding. Proverbs 17:27

God the Father, God the Son, and God the Holy Spirit,
    you made us to be in relationship.
I am frustrated. I feel misunderstood.
Give me words so they can understand
    where I'm coming from and what I need.
Give me words so they can hear that I love them.
Even if I don't feel like it right now.
Help us to listen to one another.
Help us speak kindly,
    seeking understanding
    even if we cannot agree.
Help us take joy in our differences.

85. Argument with a friend *(or family member)*

Set a guard over my mouth, O Lord; keep watch over the door of my
lips. Do not turn my heart to any evil. Psalm 141:3–4

God, keeper of all things, be with me *(and name of person)* as we
seek to understand one another. Guard our mouths and keep
watch over our lips so that we speak with kindness. Shield our
hearts from all the evil that tries to separate us. Keep watch over
us, Lord, as we seek to understand one another. *Amen.*

86. Standing up for a friend

See, I am sending you out like sheep into the midst of wolves; so be wise as serpents and innocent as doves. Matthew 10:16

My friend is being bullied.

Give me words to say what's right so that I will not just stand there when my friends are bullied.

Keep me safe.
Let me know the times I ought to speak out
and the courage to do so
and the times to be silent
and the patience to wait.

87. Healing for self, friends, or family

Just as the sufferings of Christ are abundant for us, so also our consolation is abundant through Christ. 2 Corinthians 1:5

Lord Jesus Christ, I come to you asking healing for (*name*). You carry our burdens and even suffered death on the cross so that we would have life abundantly. Hold (*name*) in your tender arms. Set her (*his/my*) body free from pain. Soothe her (*his/my*) worries. Console her (*his/my*) fears. Guide those who care for her (*him/me*). Most of all be present with (*name/me*) throughout her (*his/my*) illness. I ask this in the name of the One who draws us near, and whose compassion knows no bounds. *Amen.*

88. Loyalty

Where you go, I will go;
*   where you lodge, I will lodge;*
your people shall be my people,
*   and your God my God. Ruth 1:16*

Steadfast God, Ruth showed great loyalty to Naomi. I have
betrayed the trust between *(name)* and me. I have *(name what
is on your heart)*.

I have fallen short of the loyalty required for good, true, and
long-lasting friendships. Whenever I do wrong, I can always
return to you. I am returning now. Forgive me.

Give me strength and words, also, to return to my friend and ask
for his *(her)* forgiveness so that our friendship is not weakened
by what I have done.

Fashion in me a heart like Ruth's, a heart that is loyal to you, for
my friends and for my family. Strengthen my resolve to be loyal
to you, to my friends, and to my family.

89. Hurt by a friend

But you, O LORD, are a God merciful and gracious, slow to anger and abounding in steadfast love and faithfulness. Psalm 86:15

God, (*name*) hurt me.
I can't believe (*he/she*) betrayed me.
We are friends.
At least we *were* friends.

God, you are always merciful.
You don't get angry easily.
You are faithful.

Take my pain.
Take my anger.
Fill me with your love.

Help me know what to do.
To be patient until I'm no longer angry.
To speak to my friend truthfully.

And if possible, to be friends again.

90. Reconciliation with a friend *(or family member)*

Bear with one another and, if anyone has a complaint against another, forgive each other; just as the LORD has forgiven you, so you also must forgive. Colossians 3:13

Lord, I have not always been the best sign of your love.
I've hurt *(name of person)* and I've hurt you.

Help me to forgive myself.
Help me to return to you.

I haven't remembered that
      everything I am and have
      is a gift from you.
I'm praying to you.
Forgive me.

I will do my best to be a new person,
A better person,
Today and every day.

Give me strength to say I'm sorry to *(name of person)*.
Help us to start fresh.

91. Romantic love

[Jesus said] I give you a new commandment, that you love one another. Just as I have loved you, you also should love one another. By this everyone will know that you are my disciples, if you have love for one another. John 13:34–35

God, you love us and you ask us to love one another.

Thank you for bringing us together.
Thank you for the love we share.

Bless our love that started in friendship.
Bless the love that draws us together.

Guard our friendship.
Guide our journey.

Help us honor you by honoring one another.
Help us keep the trust we share.

May our love reflect the love you have for us.

92. Saying good-bye to a friend *(or family member)*

May the road rise up to meet you.
May the wind be always at your back.
May the sun shine warm upon your face;
the rains fall soft upon your fields and until we meet again,
may God hold you in the palm of his hand.[17]

---

17. Traditional Gaelic blessing.

93. Conversations with parents

God be in my head, and in my understanding;
God be in mine eyes, and in my looking;
God be in my mouth, and in my speaking. The Hymnal 1982 #694

Help me to know what to say
    before I speak;
Help me understand *(mom, dad, aunt, uncle, etc.)*
    before I answer;
Help me to be ready
    before I act.

Give me the strength to know
    when I need to say something,
    when I need to be silent,
    when I need to call someone for help.

Let your Holy Spirit rest upon my shoulders
    to calm me,
    to give me courage,
    and to help to take deep breaths.

I cannot face tough conversations
    and hard decisions on my own,
    without your help, O God.

Be with me.

94. Divorce or separation of parents

The human spirit will endure sickness;
but a broken spirit—
who can bear? Proverbs 18:14

God, I need you.
We are going through rough times.
My parents are not together anymore.
There is fighting, crying, worrying.
God, give me strength to get through this.

God, I need you.
I am stuck in the middle.
I am afraid of what is happening to my family.
They say they love me, but I'm not so sure.
God, give me strength to get through this.

God, I need you.
It feels like a nightmare.
There is so much anger and hurt.
Bring all of this to a calm end.
God, give me strength to get through this.

95. A new family

And in your descendants all the families of the earth shall be blessed.
Acts 3:25b

My family is changing.
(*Name*) has joined us, making us new.
It will be different. Stay with me.
Help me
    be open to new voices in the house,
    get used to sharing things in a new way,
    learn to be a new (*son, daughter, brother, sister*).
Give me
    patience when we don't understand each other,
    reassurance when I get jealous,
    comfort when I feel left out.
My family is changing.
(*Name*) has joined us, making us new.
Bless our family.

96. Death of a friend

For he will command his angels concerning you
to guard you in all your ways.
On their hands they will bear you up. Psalm 91:11–12a

Dear God, on the third day
you raised up your only son, Jesus.
Raise up my friend *(name of friend)*.
Send your angels to lift *(him/her)* up on eagle's wings.
To soar to your arms.
Keep *(him/her)* safe forever.

And send your angels to protect me.
The days are dark without my friend.
My shoulders are heavy with sadness.
My heart aches to see *(name)*.
You are my refuge and my fortress.

I don't ever want to forget *(him/her)*.
I know *(name)* is with you.
Thank you for loving us forever.

97. Death of a parent *(caregiver or loved one)*

Do not let your hearts be troubled. Believe in God, believe also in me. In my Father's house there are many dwelling-places. . . . I will come again and will take you to myself, so that where I am, there you may be also. John 14:1–3

Dear God, my father *(mother, or name)* has died.
I feel alone. Can you wrap your arms around me?
I feel empty. Can you fill me with your love?
I'm in pain. Can you soothe me with a song?

I believe in God and also in you, Jesus.
You promised that you have prepared a place.
That you will bring us to yourself.
Give me faith to know that where you are
     so is my father *(mother, or name)*.

98. Suicide of a friend

For I have no pleasure in the death of anyone, says the LORD God. Turn, then, and live. Ezekiel 18:32

There's a hole in my soul.
(*Name of friend*) was once here.
And now (*name*) is gone.

I have so many questions.
God, if you are full of love, beauty, and grace,
    why did you let this happen?

God, you share my joys,
    now share my sorrows.

Help me remember (*name of friend*),
    the good times and bad times,
    the laughter and the tears.

Welcome (*name of friend*) into your kingdom,
And care for (*his/her*) memory within me.

99. Death of a sibling

Our God is a God of salvation,
and to God, the Lord, belongs escape
from death. Psalm 68:20

Dear God, (*name of sibling*) died.
I miss her (*him*).
Even if we didn't always get along.
I miss talking.
I miss hanging out.
I even miss arguing.

I wake up in the morning. She (*he*) isn't here.
I come home. She (*he*) isn't here.
I have a joke to tell. She (*he*) isn't here.
Every day I miss her (*him*).

You raised Jesus after he died.
You conquered death.
Raise (*name of sibling*) up.
Take her (*him*) in your arms.
Hold her (*him*) tight.
Keep her (*him*) safe.

100. Death of a pet

Are not five sparrows sold for two pennies? Yet not one of them is forgotten in God's sight. Luke 12:6

Lord of all creation, I'm so sad. Comfort me.
(*Name of pet*) has been such a faithful companion,
    just like you are faithful.
(*Name of pet*) and I played and laughed,
    just like you sometimes make me laugh.
(*Name of pet*) loved me when no one else seemed to,
    just like you always love me.
(*Name of pet*) stayed with me when I was lonely,
    just like you are always with me.
Nothing can replace him (*her*).
Thank you for giving me the time to love and care for him (*her*).
Help me to continue to share kindness and care
    with all living things.

101. Homeless

He sustained him in a desert land,
  in a howling wilderness waste;
he shielded him, cared for him,
  guarded him as the apple of his eye.
Deuteronomy 32:10

We've lost our home, God.
We don't have anyplace to live.
We're in the wilderness.
A howling wasteland.

No warm bed to sleep in.
No shower to wash up.
No washer or dryer to clean our clothes.
No place to do my homework.
Nothing I can call just my own.
We need to ask for food.
I'm so embarrassed.

Why did this happen?
Where are you?
Why have you deserted us?

God, you gave Mary a place to rest.
Give us a place to rest too.
Shield us and care for us.
Guard us as the apple of your eye.

102. Moving to a new town, city, or home

Unless the LORD builds the house, those who build it labor in vain.
Unless the LORD guards the city, the guard keeps watch in vain.
Psalm 127:1

I am somewhere new.

I seek your guidance and your goodness.
    So much is different:
    new places, new people, new questions, new worries.

Help me to see this move as a new adventure,
    with hope and anticipation of:
    new friendships, new activities, new things to learn.

Thank you for (*names of household members*)
    as we face the new days ahead together:
    unpacking, finding our way, getting settled.

Be with me in my comings and goings,
    send your angels to watch over and protect me,
    and all whom I love:
    my family, my friends left behind, my new friends to come.

I am somewhere new and I know . . . you are still with me.

School and Work

*An educated person knows many things,
and one with much experience knows what
he is talking about.*
Sirach 34:9

103. Beginnings

In the beginning was the Word, and the Word was with God, and the Word was God. He was in the beginning with God. All things came into being through him and without him not one thing came into being. John 1:1–3a

God, you were present at the beginning.
Be with me as I begin (*a new school year, new job, college*).
Comfort me when I am unsure of my new surroundings.
Strengthen me when I stumble,
And help me remember that your light shines in all places.
All this I ask through you, my Creator, Redeemer, and Sustainer.

104. Athletics

Do you know that in a race the runners compete, but only one receives the prize? Run in such a way that you may win it. Athletes exercise self-control in all things; they do it to receive a perishable wreath, but we an imperishable one. 1 Corinthians 9:24–25

Dear God,
Hold me in your loving hands.
Look after me and protect me
    as I travel and compete.
Give me courage, honor, strength,
    good sportsmanship, and skill.
Help me believe that through your power
    I can do anything.
As long as I keep my faith, I can finish any race.

105. Before a performance

Raise a song, sound the tambourine,
the sweet lyre with the harp. Psalm 81:2

God, you give us more than we can dream or hope for.
Thank you for all the people who contributed to this event.
Bless their gifts, their commitment, and their work.
Bless (*name directors, teachers, fellow performers, etc.*).
Thank you for the opportunity to share my joy.

May it raise song and make merry hearts
among those gathered to share
the joy in your creation.

May our success not be measured by
winning or losing, perfection or imperfection,
but by your perfect joy in creation.

106. Exams

All must test their own work; then that work, rather than their
neighbor's work, will become a cause for pride. Galatians 6:4

Jesus, be with me.
I've studied long and hard.
Thank you for the skills I've learned.
Give me confidence to use them.
Jesus, help me through this challenge.
I'll do my best with you at my side.
Thank you.

107. Being bullied

Protect me from my enemies and keep me safe from those who lay in wait for me. Wisdom 10:12a (adapted)

I'm scared to go to school.
I'm hurting.
I'm afraid.
I have no place to turn.
So I am turning to you.

They are calling me names.
Give me strength to tell them to stop.
Protect me from my enemies.

They are pushing me around.
Help me walk away.
Protect me from my enemies.

Give me a safe place to go.
Where I won't be taunted.
Protect me from my enemies.

They are saying mean things about me.
Help me stand up for myself.
Protect me from my enemies.

Help me make friends I can trust.
So we can stick together.
Protect me from my enemies.

Keep me safe.

108. Violence in school

But you, O Lord, do not be far away!
O my help, come quickly to my aid! Psalm 22:19

Lord Jesus Christ, our Savior and great protector,
    come and help us.

People in my school are filled with harshness and hatred.
They tease, bully, fight, shun, and cut others down.
My school is not safe.
Sometimes I'm afraid.
Be with me. Be with all of us.
Protect me. Protect all of us.

Be with those who are doing the violence too.
Help them to see that violence will only bring more violence.
I don't know why they act out. You do. Help them.

Protect my school. Students, teachers,
coaches, principals, guidance counselors,
those who work in the lunchroom,
those who keep the school clean.
Everyone. Keep us safe.

109. Facing a difficult day

When you pass through the waters, I will be with you; and through the rivers, they shall not overwhelm you. Isaiah 43:2a

I'm feeling overwhelmed.
So much to squeeze into one day.
So much to get done.
Am I ready for the challenge?
For a new day at school?
I'm not sure.
You are my God.
Be with me.
It's going to be a tough one.

110. Beginning a new job

Let the favor of the Lord our God be upon us, and prosper for us the work of our hands—O prosper the work of our hands! Psalm 90:17

Be with me today.

I'm beginning a new job.
I'm nervous and excited too.
Calm my nerves and share my excitement.

Bless my hands.
Bless my mind.
Bless my heart.
Bless my work.

Be with me today.

111. Homework

Whatever your task, put yourselves into it, as done for the LORD and not for your masters. Colossians 3:23

God of wisdom and might, you set before us good tasks.
My teacher(s) have given me this work for learning.
Sit beside me so that I might persevere through this work's end.
Focus my mind with calm resolve to bring my self to the task.
Enliven my mind to learn, question, and challenge what I do.

112. Applying for a job *(or apprenticeship)*

Now to him who by the power at work within us is able to accomplish abundantly far more than all we can ask or imagine, to him be glory in the church and in Christ Jesus to all generations, forever and ever. Amen. Ephesians 3:20–21

God who gives us more than we ask,
You have given me many talents.
I come to you with humility.
Bless this application.
Guide my hand to present myself with confidence and truth.
Grant me words to speak my strength and skills.
Be present during the interview to calm my nerves.
Open the eyes and ears of those who read my application.
Even if this is not the right job and I am not hired,
I know you give us more than we ask.
Glory to you, Lord Jesus Christ.
Glory to you.

113. First paying job

For we are what he has made us, created in Christ Jesus for good
works, which God prepared beforehand to be our way of life.
Ephesians 2:10

Praise to you for the work you do in all our lives.
Praise to you for preparing good work for me to do.
Praise to you for the ability to do that work.
Praise to you for guiding (*name of business or person*)
    who hired me.

Support me in this, my first job.
Replace my fears with expectation of good things.
Build up my confidence to apply my abilities.

May this work proclaim your goodness.
May it build your kingdom.
May it be a blessing to you.

God, I dedicate my work to you.

114. Losing a job

Teach me to do your will,
for you are my God.
Let your good spirit lead me
on a level path. Psalm 143:10

God, you are my God.
I have lost my job.

Where shall I go?
To whom can I turn?
I can turn to you, God.
I can go where you call.

God, you are my God.
Restore my confidence.
Help me to see that I am good.

Lord God, I turn to you.
Provide a new path for me.
Lead me to new opportunities
to do your will in this world.

Community and World

And he said to them, "Go into all the world and
proclaim the good news to the whole creation."
  Mark 16:15

115. Basic education

Let the wise also hear and gain in learning,
and the discerning acquire skill. Proverbs 1:5

Thank you for giving me the opportunity to go to school.
There are many like me who don't have a classroom, books,
      or a place to study.
There are many who come to school hungry and tired.
Hear my prayer.

Let those who make decisions about programs and funding
      be fair to all students.
Provide teachers and classrooms for those who are
      hungry to learn.
Watch over all those who teach and those who learn,
      and those who wish they could.
Hear my prayer.

116. Poverty

Speak out for those who cannot speak, for the rights of the destitute.
Speak out, judge righteously, defend the rights of the poor and needy.
Proverbs 31:8–9

God of power and strength,
      we are waiting for the coming of your Kingdom
      when there will be no hunger, no sickness, no one in need.
Help us to bring your Kingdom closer each day
      by serving those who are seen as the least in our society
      and working toward justice for every person.
For when we serve them, we are serving you.

117. Children of the world

A voice was heard in Ramah, wailing and loud lamentation, Rachel weeping for her children; she refused to be consoled, because they are no more. Matthew 2:18

I see the pictures on the news,
    in magazines
    and on the Internet.
Mothers crying,
    holding lifeless children,
    their bodies covered with flies.
Why God?

They are in another world,
    but come to my world
    through images of pain and suffering;
I feel helpless,
    their pain becomes my pain
    and I am but one person.
Why God?

Show me ways to make a difference,
    the little things that I can do
    so I can help those who seem more helpless than me.
How God? Show me how.

118. The environment

For the LORD is a great God, and a great King above all gods. In his hands are the depths of the earth; the heights of the mountains are his also. The sea is his, for he made it, and the dry land, which his hands have formed. Psalm 95:3–5

God, you are a great God, greater than all gods.
In your hands are all the corners of the earth.
You made majestic mountains.
You made the deep sea and all that lives in it.
You prepared the dry land for beasts, bugs, and birds.
And you brought us into your creation.

You called us to tend the land.
But we have lived for ourselves only.
We have abused creation. Contaminated the rivers.
Polluted the air. Spoiled the soil.
We have forgotten that all of creation is yours.

Have mercy on us.
Open our eyes to the ways we hurt the world.
Transform our indifference into compassion.
Move us to change our hurtful ways.
Make us bold to do what is needed,
knowing that we cannot do it alone,
only through your grace.

119. Clean water

I will sprinkle clean water upon you. Ezekiel 36:25a

God, you create all the waters that cover the earth;
    Oceans, rivers, lakes, and streams,
    Rain, sleet, hail, and snow.
Water is life and gives life;
    Wells, cisterns, water holes, and reservoirs,
    Sanitation, water treatment, and potable water.

Help us to clean up your creation
    so that all people might have water that gives life.
You baptized us with your living water.
Let us provide life-giving water to others.

120. End to war

He shall judge between the nations, and shall arbitrate for many peoples; they shall beat their swords into plowshares, and their spears into pruning hooks; nation shall not lift up sword against nation, neither shall they learn war any more. Isaiah 2:4

God of Peace,
Open the eyes of those who want to dominate others
through violence, oppression, hatred, and ignorance.

Help the leaders of all nations see that peace
will make a better world for today's youth
and tomorrow's children.

121. Gender equality

So God created humankind in his image, in the image of God he created them; male and female he created them. Genesis 1:27

Male and female
God, you made us in your image.
You gave us life
and you know each of us from the inside and outside.
Help me recognize the equal value of men and women.

Equal respect
Male and female

Male and female
We are special in your eyes.
You gave us unique abilities
and celebrate our diversity and creativity.
Help me recognize that gender doesn't change a person's value.

Equal worth
Male and female

Male and female
Help me to be responsible for my behavior toward others
and be a supporter for gender equality
in school, work, and sports
so that male and female
will all have equal value, equal respect, equal worth.

Equally made
Male and female

122. Hunger

For I was hungry and you gave me food, I was thirsty and you gave
me something to drink. I was a stranger and you welcomed me.
Matthew 25:35

God, the world is hungry.
People starving in Africa, their ribs are showing
    and their stomachs are bloated.
The man on the corner holds a cardboard sign asking for food.
Children go to school without breakfast
    and to bed without dinner.

God, sometimes I am hungry.
My stomach rumbles, and I look at the clock to see the time.
I know I will eat sometime today.

God, the world is hungry.
Bring comfort to those who do not know
    where their next meal is coming from.
Give strength to relief agencies that bring hope
    to those who suffer famine.
Provide patience to those who work in soup kitchens.
Nudge me to do my part to provide for others.
With your help, we can be united to feed the world.

123. Peace

Blessed are the peacemakers, for they will be called children of God.
Matthew 5:9

Help me to be an instrument of your peace
    by listening to others before I speak against them,
    by learning about others before I judge them,
    by remembering what Jesus would have done.

Help me to be an instrument of your peace
    by talking through disagreements,
    by seeking help from others,
    by turning the other cheek.

Help me to be an instrument of your peace
    by promoting nonviolent actions,
    by advocating for peace in my community,
    by praying for peace in the world.

124. Political oppression

Learn to do good; seek justice, rescue the oppressed, defend the
orphan, plead for the widow. Isaiah 1:17

Lord, we are your voice in the world today.
Help us to speak out when we see injustice.
Give us courage to fight for the rights of others.
Watch over those being held as political prisoners.
Keep those who are afraid, strong in their faith in you.
For your ways of peace and love will overcome all evil.

125. World disease

*For I will restore health to you, and your wounds I will heal, says the
LORD. Jeremiah 30:17a*

Our world is ravaged by disease.
Give strength to doctors, nurses, and all
    who take care of the sick.
Provide energy and determination to all who are looking for
    cures for HIV/AIDS and cancer.
Open the minds of all your people to learn new ways
    that will help them stay healthy.

Help our countries to work together to eradicate all diseases
    so that all children will know their parents
    and all parents can watch their children grow up.

Prayer Index

Scripture Index